Why take this book seriously?

Here's what Best Men who have been coached by the author have to say…

"Feedback from all was amazing. The preparation and structure for my Best Man Speech gave me the confidence to improvise on the day. Was very natural. Thanks for your help, very grateful."

— Mike Morris, Best Man

"Huge thanks – the content refinements and suggestions you gave me in your eCritique were unbelievably helpful. Big, big thanks."

— Pete Wilson, Best Man

"Speech couldn't have gone better. Lots of laughs and a standing ovation at the end!"

— Ben Smart, Best Man

"After my speech, I was inundated with people saying it was the best they had heard. Going to the time and effort of doing it properly really paid dividends."

— Stephen Newman, Best Man

"My identical twin brother asked me to be his Best Man, so I knew I had to deliver an extremely funny, intelligent and, most importantly, personal speech for him. The pressure was on...

A friend told me about Simon Bucknall and how good he was. I was intrigued. From the first time I spoke to Simon, I knew it was the right decision... At the wedding, I got absolutely rave reviews but the biggest compliment was the wedding photographer coming up to me afterwards to say that [my speech] was the best he'd ever heard!"

— Oliver Westray, Best Man

"Helped me improve my confidence and, as a result, I was able to enjoy my best friend's wedding without worrying about speaking in front of 140 guests."

— Tom Freeman, Best Man

"People were even coming up to me the day after to congratulate me on the speech. One groom-to-be has even requested me to be the Best Man at his wedding, due in the next year or so. Well done and thanks."

— Danny Cunningham, Best Man

the art of connect
ion

THE BEST MAN SPEAKER
THE DEFINITIVE GUIDE

Simon Bucknall

ANTE BIBENDI, LOQUENDI

THE BEST MAN SPEAKER the definitive guide

the art of connect ion

Text ©2014 Simon Bucknall

THE BEST MAN SPEAKER the definitive guide
Published by The Art Of Connection
The Limes, 1339 High Road, London N20 9HR
www.theartofconnection.co.uk
Tel +44 (0)7834 083500

Version 1.0

Designed by Ayd Instone, www.sunmakers.co.uk
Illustrations by Marty Jessup, Elephants Can't Jump.
Edited by Eileen Cathcart, The Art Of Connection.
Author photo by John Cassidy.

ISBN: 978-1-910347-02-7

www.theartofconnection.co.uk

To William Rowe

The Groom who entrusted me

Contents

Foreword
by Andreas Kalavanas
Owner, Moxhull Hall Hotel

As a hotelier, I have personally undertaken the planning and delivery of more than fifteen hundred weddings. So, I know how important the speeches can be in making a good day become a 'great wedding'.

I've seen literally thousands of wedding speeches. Some were tremendous. There was laughter, emotion and applause aplenty. But too many of the speeches have been *agonising.* In some cases, I simply had to leave the room because the Best Man crumbled. I've seen Best Men lock themselves in toilets through fear. I've seen them unable to eat due to nerves. I've seen Best Men speak for as long as an hour… and as little as 30 seconds.

Some are overconfident. They think they can wing it… and they can't. Others think they're funny… but they're not. Still others think it's all about being as crude as possible… which it certainly is not! I've heard the same tired internet gags reeled off time and again.

With all this experience, you might think that when I was asked to be a Best Man, I'd be in great shape. My nearest and dearest assumed giving the Best Man Speech would be no problem at all.

Wrong.

I was absolutely terrified. All I could think about were the great speeches I'd heard and the knowledge that I could never deliver anything close. I was convinced that I'd only ever be remembered for the terrible speech I'd go on to make at my best friend's wedding.

With a full year to prepare and being a pretty confident guy (normally), the prospect of delivering a speech to 180 guests filled me with horror.

I started with the internet. Not knowing what else to do, why not seek out some useful advice online? I was about to give up but then... I found Simon. It was his speech on YouTube that did it for me. If you haven't watched it, then stop reading until you have done. Because you should.

It wasn't long before I made my decision. I needed help and Simon was the man. He became my Best Man Speaker Coach.

With Simon's help, I'm pleased to say that my speech was a huge success. I even *enjoyed* giving it. Guests at the wedding simply could not believe how good it was. To this day, people still come up to me and say it was the best speech they had ever heard at a wedding. One guest even invited me to be an after-dinner speaker at a charity event – extraordinary!

Most importantly, my best friend and new bride were elated. They knew how scared I'd been and what it took for me to go through with the speech.

What did Simon do that made a difference?

He gave me the belief that I could actually do it. He helped me create content that was relevant, structured and effective. Crucially, he helped me identify and hone material I felt comfortable with. He taught me delivery techniques that were so practical and simple that I was able to deliver the speech with confidence.

You'll find these techniques explored in depth during the course of this book. Take on board the ideas and *they will* transform the impact of your speech.

There's no doubt in my mind that Simon got me through that wedding day. I felt ready, trained and confident. Most of all, it felt so good delivering a speech congruent with who I am. It was about me as a Best Man Speaker, rather than just parroting someone else's speech.

Not a single person in that room thought I was acting or had even practised. They just saw me as who I am. Simon didn't try to 'remould' my character. He simply worked with what he had and helped bring out the best in me. That ten minute speech had a massive impact on me. I finally conquered one of my deepest fears – for that I have Simon to thank.

Enjoy what you're about read – and most important, apply what you learn!

www.moxhullhall.co.uk

Quick start guide

6 steps to construct the core of your speech in 15 minutes...

1. Put any speech notes, drafts and emails to one side where you can't see them.

2. Pour yourself a drink, put some music on and have a think about The Groom – what's his single Greatest Quality?

3. How do you know that Quality is true of The Groom? What have you seen him do, say or experience? Jot down your ideas.

4. Which THREE further Key Qualities (good or bad) do you think characterise The Groom?

5. How do you know each of these Key Qualities is truly characteristic of The Groom? What have you seen him do, say or experience?

6. Make a note of your ideas, especially any *stories* which come to mind. They don't have to be funny – all that matters is that they are *true* of The Groom.

If you follow this simple process, you'll quickly construct the backbone to your Best Man Speech: three 'Key Qualities' (each illustrated by relevant experience) which form the heart of your speech, followed by a single 'Greatest Quality' which anchors the conclusion of your speech, just before you Toast The Couple.

Welcome and introduction

Now then, be honest.

How are you feeling?

Chances are if you're reading this, you have a Best Man Speech to develop and deliver. At the very least, you're likely to know someone who does.

The Best Man Speech at a wedding is important. Guests eagerly anticipate the speech and they expect it to be entertaining.

As a Best Man Speaker, delivering a cracking speech is a tough ask. Mainly, this is due to the pressure of audience expectations, which perhaps explains the vast array of advice available on the internet: from speech templates to plug-in gags, from speech openings to cute turns of phrase, to video samples and the rest.

There's only one problem.

Much of the advice available on the internet isn't terribly helpful... unless, that is, you're happy for someone else to tell you what to say in one of the most important speeches of your life.

Over the past few years, I've spoken to countless Best Men about their experience of preparing their speech. The vast majority complain that most of the so-called 'advice' on offer amounts to little more than 'just-say-this-and-you'll-be-ok'.

This book is different.

You see, the problem with the 'just-say-this-and-you'll-be-ok' approach is that it compromises the authenticity of your speech. Why would you want to use someone else's material for a speech as personal, heartfelt and special as a speech at the wedding of one of your closest friends?

There's an obsession with 'good gags' when it comes to Best Man speech advice on the web. You could be forgiven for thinking that all you need do is jot down some crude one-liners on a bunch of flashcards, take a few deep breaths, humiliate The Groom and let the audience do the rest.

Some sources of wisdom even offer a fully written model script! Just fill in the blanks, make a few tweaks and Presto! You're guaranteed a successful outcome.

Sounds like plagiarism to me.

From my perspective, not only as a professional speaker but also as a Best Man and as a *coach* to innumerable Best Men, the best speeches, including the best *Best Man Speeches*, are personal.

More importantly, they're authentic. They're true to *who* you are and how you feel about two important people in your life.

If you want to deliver a first-class speech, we need to focus on developing your skills as a *speaker*.

Forget cutting-and-pasting some else's text. Focus on improving your skills as a speaker and you'll deliver a better speech. What's more, you'll feel much, much better about it too!

Take on board the tips contained within this book and you'll gain a level of communications insight and practical expertise which you can also take forward into the rest of your life, whether you're presenting in the workplace, in meetings or simply engaging people in everyday chit-chat.

While this book does contain concrete advice on how to prepare, structure, populate and deliver your speech, the actual content itself must come from you. Not me.

Does this mean it'll take a bit of time and effort?

Of course.

But believe me, it'll be worth it in the long run.

Once a Best Man, always a Best Man.

Chances are, this is a speech you'll remember for the rest of your life. At the very least, it's a speech which the Bride and Groom will remember. Members of the wedding *audience* will also likely be talking about it for a long time too.

Wouldn't it be great for them to talk about your speech for the right reasons?

Huge amounts of money are spent nowadays on weddings. Check out any wedding magazine or fair and you'll see an extraordinary array of outfits, flower arrangements, venue options, gift ideas and more. Yet very little is made available by way of quality support for the speakers. This, despite the fact that the speeches will be among the most memorable aspects of the day.

I'm not saying the speeches are the *most* important thing. What I am saying is that some extra time, effort and expertise invested in the development and delivery of your wedding speech will reap dividends for a magical day.

With that in mind, think of this book as your personal guide. Together, we'll look at a simple, practical and actionable process for developing and delivering a cracking Best Man Speech which will delight your audience. The end product will be 100% yours, without recourse to cutting-and-pasting stale gags off the internet.

Think of the journey as a *speaker's* journey. Of course we'll map out and explore the relevant segments of your speech as we go. The process is one which will accelerate your development as a person, so that you start to think, feel and behave as a *speaker* behaves, rather than being programmed to regurgitate someone else's gags.

Along the way, we'll take a look at additional points of interest, including specific tips and insights which will be of value not just for your Best Man Speech but for any presentation you deliver in the future.

Will the result be a Best Man Speech that's funny?

More than likely.

More importantly, if you employ the keys outlined in this book, your speech will be *authentic*. It'll be a speech you can look back on with pride and satisfaction for the rest of your life.

To help you achieve this, you'll benefit not only from my experience of coaching countless Best Men in recent years, but also from my first-hand experience of the professional speaking world.

I say this not to try to impress you. Rather I want to reassure you that, when it comes to public speaking, I've 'been there and done it'. The ideas contained within this book are rooted in *first-hand experience* coaching not only a significant number of Best Men but also a vast array of high-achieving professionals, leaders and opinion formers from all walks of life across more than a dozen countries. This includes not only wedding speakers, but also corporate executives, charity workers, refugees, politicians, academics, prison inmates, police officers, MBAs, teachers and teenagers in schools.

Back in August 2007, I gave a Best Man Speech at the wedding of a very close school friend of mine. The Groom, bless him, took the liberty of saying in *his* speech:

"By the way, Simon is a championship-winning speaker. And in just four weeks time he'll be representing the UK and Ireland in the finals of the World Championship of Public Speaking in America, for the second year running. So he'll be really good!"

Gee, thanks. No pressure then.

You'll access the best advice I can offer drawn from that experience. You'll also pick up specific skills I developed on my journey to representing the UK & Ireland twice in the finals of the World Championship of Public Speaking in 2006 and 2007.

Let's look briefly at what you can expect to get from this book.

As you and I will almost certainly never have met before, I'm acutely aware that you could be at any point along the 'comfort spectrum' in terms of your speech. You may be feeling anxious and having to start from scratch. Or you may be at the opposite extreme and feel really quite confident, simply looking for some tips to help you fine-tune your script and performance. You may, of course, be somewhere in between.

Be assured, wherever you are with your speech, if you're taking it seriously and have an open mind, you'll find this book useful.

Take a look at the following common issues/questions:

- If all I've got is a blank sheet of paper, where do I even start?

- How do I structure my speech for maximum impact?

- What if I can't think of any good stories to use?

- What if my stories about The Groom aren't funny?

- How do I know which stories to use?

- How do I avoid being cheesy?

- What do I do about nervousness?

- What about the practicalities?

- Should I use notes or not?

- How do I speak without notes?

- What about microphones? Staging? Rehearsing?

This book provides practical advice for tackling all of the above.

All that's necessary on *your* part is a sincere commitment to doing the best possible job as Best Man for The Groom. Your willingness to try some things which may seem a bit weird, even counter-intuitive, will also come in handy.

I should add that just reading this book puts you way ahead of the pack. Most Best Men, if they do any research at all, simply pull material off the internet and sprinkle it through their speech, assuming that all will be well.

Big mistake.

By investing both time and money in this book, my promise to you is that you'll get the best that I can offer – and it will make a difference.

A quick logistical point:

As we work our way through this book, from time to time I'll refer to the Best Man Speech I gave back in the summer of 2007.

Again, this is not my way of trying to impress you.

Rather it's to provide you with concrete examples of how the techniques we explore *can actually work* when speaking in front of a live audience.

You'll also see *how and why* I did the things I did. Thankfully, audience feedback suggested the speech went down well, although you can watch and judge this for yourself!

Either way, I suggest you will find it helpful to view the speech on Youtube. It'll take you less than 10 minutes. Just search under:

'simon bucknall best man speech'

OR

http://www.theartofconnection.co.uk/how_to_give_a_best_man_speech.html

I'll also quote relevant excerpts from my original Best Man Speech script. The full script is contained in the Appendix below so watching the video is not essential, but by viewing it you'll see how the audience responded on the day, which is important. I'll include a time reference in square brackets e.g. [5:30 mins] at the beginning of each of the quotes so you can find the relevant section in the video as quickly and easily as possible.

Some early words of reassurance

The book is structured around **7 Keys** to developing and delivering a cracking Best Man Speech. Before we go into the 1st Key, let me offer you a few further words of reassurance.

You may or may not be feeling anxious about your speech. Either way, many of the Best Men I talk to find the prospect daunting. This is not through any fault of their own but because of the pressure and weight of *other people's expectations*.

Can you relate to that?

It's the pressure to be engaging; the pressure to be the highlight of the Wedding Breakfast; above all, the pressure to be funny.

Believe me, if you feel that or you've been feeling it, you're in good company.

When I was Best Man, The Groom teasingly mentioned the World Championship of Public Speaking Finals. Quite deliberately, he wanted to set an audience expectation I could have well done without.

Have a think about the expectations you feel under for your speech. Who are the people that come to mind? Which of your friends come to mind?

The reason I ask is because how you focus your mind's

attention when preparing your speech is vitally important. Misplaced focus is responsible for one of the single biggest mistakes I see Best Men make and, believe me, I've seen a lot of speeches both live and online.

The mistake they make is this:

They focus on making their friends laugh.

Now, why is that a mistake?

Well, imagine for a moment that you're the Father-of-The-Bride.

You've just given away your beautiful daughter... one of the great joys of your life, the apple of your eye... and you've given her to a man you *desperately* hope will take good care of her and make her happy.

Right?

Imagine the intensity of your emotions.

And imagine the emotions of the Mother-of-The-Bride, discreetly wiping a tear as she remembers her own childhood days dreaming of that magical moment when her Prince Charming would come...

Then up steps some prat (supposedly your new son-in-law's *closest* friend) who tells everyone that The Groom is a complete idiot.

To cap it all, this is happening at an event in which you, as Parents of The Bride, may well have invested *thousands of pounds.*

How would you feel?

My point is this:

Your Best Man Speech is not about your friends.

It's not even about The Groom's friends.

It's for the whole audience, but most of all for The Parents of The Bride.

Why?

Because no Best Man ever gave a great speech by making The Groom's friends cheer...and The Bride's Parents cry.

There are some truly awful Best Man speeches out there. Just run a few searches on YouTube. What they typically have in common is a talent for making the viewer cringe.

These are the product of what I call the 'Weak Man Speaker' – the speaker who makes all the classic mistakes when preparing his speech.

Typically, the Weak Man Speaker begins his research on the

internet. He goes trawling for cheap material, digs out a few lurid stories about The Groom getting drunk, being sick and shagging Olga the Bulgarian shot-putter on a big night out (no offence intended to Eastern European female field athletes).

Internet gags fall flat because audiences have an unerring ability to spot they've been lifted, especially since they'll probably have heard the joke before. Crudity usually falls flat because half the audience feels offended, while the other half is busy worrying about the first half.

It may just be me, but if internet gags and crudity are the best a 'Best' Man can do, that says more about him than The Groom.

To avoid Weak Man Speaker status and ensure that you go down as a true Best Man Speaker, then take these two core messages to heart and you'll be well on your way:

First: being hilarious is a bonus. Making The Parents proud is essential. You'll see how you can do that in the very 1st Key below.

Secondly: steer clear of jokes taken off the internet. Focus on developing personal, authentic material that's true both to you and The Groom. That way, you're much more likely to achieve a strong connection with the audience.

Relax about having to write 'something funny' early on in the development of your speech. It's not about inserting jokes.

Your best humour will be uncovered later. Give it time…

That's why we won't be covering humour until the 6th Key.

OK?

Still with me?

If so, then great!

Let's get cracking and begin the journey to developing you as a Best Man Speaker…

Simon Bucknall

🔑 The 1st Key

Where to begin

You may already have some initial ideas and a rough draft… or you may not. But let's assume for argument's sake that you're starting with a blank page.

Erm…so, where do you start?

Answer: not at the beginning.

Nor should you begin by going on the internet in search of 'stock jokes' or openings.

Trying to write the opening to a speech from scratch is extremely difficult and best avoided. Very often, speakers put off even preparing their speech for that very reason – because it's so tricky to do.

Equally, cutting and pasting someone else's material is a problem because it clutters your thinking and risks compromising your authenticity, right from the start. Don't get me wrong: the internet can be a useful resource a little bit later on (for checking out other speeches, getting an idea of what works and what doesn't, perhaps even seeking out a coach!) but I'm just saying it's a poor place to search for actual speech material.

Recently, I was coaching a Best Man who had sent a few emails to some friends. The problem was this resulted in lots of little bits and pieces coming back. He had too many disconnected fragments, making it difficult to lay the foundations for his speech.

So, how should you start the process?

My advice is that you dedicate time to some Quality Thinking & Quality Conversations.

The good news is this means NO SCRIPTING... yet.

In my experience, conversations are an important part of the early speech development process. Not only will you gather valuable intelligence about The Groom, but also conversations quickly help you to clarify your own thinking.

Partly this is because interacting with a fellow human being is a far more dynamic way of stimulating speech ideas than staring at a blank screen or sheet of paper. It's also more enjoyable – depending on whom you're talking to!

To make things nice and easy, however, I suggest we start by having you clear your head and having a little chat with yourself.

So, let's limber up by doing some Quality Thinking...

Quality thinking

Forget everyone else for a moment. Put them to the back of your mind and just have a think about what you want to say about The Groom.

I mean...*really* say. From a *positive* point of view.

Specifically, what do you feel is his greatest asset - his greatest strength? Or, as we'll be calling it in this book, his 'Great Gift'.

Guaranteed, there'll be something. And yes, this should be sincere. This is not about cracking jokes. You need to really mean this. Be assured, we'll come to the funny stuff later.

You may find it helpful to do something else at the same time so your mind can wander. Perhaps listen to some music, pour yourself a drink (as advised in the Quick Start Guide), go for a drive or go for a run. Personally, I find many of my best ideas come when out for a jog.

Get as clear and single-minded as you can about The Groom's Great Gift. Perhaps it's his sense of fun…or maybe his ability to put others at ease…or perhaps his loyalty to his friends and family…

In the case of my Best Man Speech, 'loyalty' was the quality I really wanted to focus on. Based on sixteen years of knowing Will, I believed that was his 'Great Gift', the one quality above all others which I wanted to convey to the audience.

It also happened to be one I felt The Parents would appreciate, for obvious reasons!

During this Quality Thinking, you may identify other observations about The Groom which are less serious…or less complimentary. That's great. Jot them down for later.

Giving serious thought to The Groom's Great Gift at this early stage is vital. It gives you clarity and, more importantly, an 'anchor' for your speech. Think of it as a point of certainty which you can work towards. More on that later.

The Gift is not something you'll necessarily want to reference early on in your speech. Indeed, quite the opposite. More often than not, you'll want to reveal the 'Groom's Great Gift' towards the end of the speech, given its heartfelt nature.

You may think it odd not to 'begin at the beginning' of your speech. Trust me. Leave your speech opening until later. Speech openings are so much easier to prepare provided you've established what you want to say.

Once you have this Gift clear in your mind, let's take the next step and have a think about *other* key qualities which you feel characterise The Groom.

These could be positive – but they might equally be negative!

Just make a list at this stage. Relax about whether you feel you have 'funny material'. Just get up to three, say, Key Qualities which relate to The Groom and which are nice and clear in your mind.

Many Best Men make the mistake of just launching into conversations with friends and family without giving it any thought first. The problem with pinging out an email saying: 'Anyone got any good stories about The Groom?' is that people don't know how to help you. Giving a blank canvas like that makes it surprisingly difficult for people to come up with useful, specific and relevant material.

By doing some Quality Thinking in advance, you're more likely to have productive conversations with people because you already have a framework to guide your thinking.

For example, on my list of Qualities of The Groom, I had:

- Laziness

- Salesy

- Mischief-maker (especially at school)

- Good fun

- Lover of science-fiction

- A keen reader

- Drama queen

Your list will obviously be different. Think of it as your first cut at outlining the 'backbone' for your speech – because as we'll see, an effective Best Man Speech consists of making a series of observations about the Groom (whether serious or humorous), backed up by relevant stories.

Use the draft list of Key Qualities to help guide your Conversations which follow (see below). People will want to help you, but that can be difficult if they have no idea what you're really after.

You may find that as you talk to people, quality material just flows easily. But if you introduce specific Qualities of The Groom which you're looking to explore, it's much easier for them to recall stories which you might use. Without this guidance, there's also the risk they default to the 'most obvious story' which may or may not be useful for you, especially if it means you end up with six 'do-you-remember-the-time-when-he-threw-up-all-over-the-bathroom' stories!

That's why it's vital to do the Quality Thinking *before* you enter into...

Conversation 1: The Groom

You may think I'm bonkers but I strongly recommend that you talk to The Groom *early* in the speech development process.

You'd be amazed how often Best Men don't think to do this. Usually that's because Best Men think everything should be kept deathly secret.

Again, please don't misunderstand me here. I'm not saying you should tell him what you're going to say. (How could you? You haven't even written the speech yet!) The object of the exercise is to get his input into the speech *parameters*, particularly around his expectations.

Partly that's because it's the polite thing to do. After all, he's granted you the rare privilege of being his Best Man and you have a responsibility to do right by him.

Why not ask about his hopes and desires for the big day? Believe me, he'll appreciate your asking. You may even find him to be pleasantly surprised that you took the trouble.

More importantly, talking with The Groom gives you an opportunity to establish some boundaries. Think of them as ground rules. Professional speakers check for potential taboo subjects with clients before a gig. Why not do the same with your speech?

It will reap dividends for you because it helps protect you against the risk of unintentionally dropping a clanger during the speech. You know the one: where the audience takes a sharp intake of breath and everyone feels terribly awkward? Yes, that.

Useful questions you might consider asking The Groom include:

- What (if any) family politics/sensitivities should I be aware of?

- Are there any particularly important people I should mention?

- Is there anyone you know who'd like to be at the wedding but can't make it?

- Are there any taboo subjects?

This last question is particularly important because you offend your audience at your peril!

REMEMBER: No Best Man gave a cracking speech by making The Parents cry!

One very successful professional speaker I know in the USA breaks the ice with his audiences by joking about his journey to the venue, which often involves flying.

However, I remember hearing him tell the story of how, on one occasion, checking for taboo subjects with his client beforehand, he was informed:

"Whatever you do, don't talk about flying...two of our company directors were killed in a plane crash last year."

Imagine what might have happened if the speaker hadn't gained this vital piece of intelligence in advance?

A while back, I was coaching a Best Man who, when he talked to The Groom, was told:

"Please DO NOT reference the age gap between me and The Bride. Trust me, we've heard all the jokes before. We simply don't need to hear them on our Wedding Day."

If you are serious about doing a good job, why risk treading on a taboo?

Talking to The Groom is also a useful opportunity to get his side of some stories you may wish to include in your speech, such as:

- How did The Groom first meet The Bride...what happened?

- Where did he propose...and what happened?

- How was the first meeting with The Bride's Parents/Family?

This may give you some good material for use later on, especially when you contrast his side of the story with that of other people. In particular, you may have fun comparing his description of the proposal with The Bride's perspective, since you'll be talking to her next!

So...

Conversation 2: The Bride

Time to talk to the lady of the hour.

Again, be sure to check expectations and taboo subjects, even if you feel you know The Bride and Groom very well, as you never know what may be lurking in the background...

It's definitely worth asking how she first met The Groom. When it comes to developing your content later on, the stories of how they met and of the marriage proposal are guaranteed to interest the audience...plus of course, you're likely to be on safe ground.

Relax about whether you feel the material you're getting at this stage is 'funny'. It doesn't have to be.

It *really* doesn't have to be.

Just record whatever you think is relevant and true. Further down the line, you'll be surprised how material which at first glance can appear dull, actually proves to be entertaining for the wedding audience.

In my own Best Man Speech, I began by talking about the time when The Groom first told me about Hannah, his Bride-to-be. On the face of it, not a hilarious story, but later I found a way to make it entertaining for the audience.

There's a good chance you'll find the same. But don't rush it. Humour is something you unearth rather than insert!

Record as much as you can from these two vital conversations, whether written, electronic or audio record.

It's been said that the difference between a good comedian and a great comedian is a notebook and a pen. The same might be said of speakers.

Your records don't have to be pretty, but you do want to jot down as much as you can. You never know when the information might come in useful.

Remember: these conversations are about raw intelligence gathering, not scripting.

Conversation 3: The Family

Have a chat with a few well-chosen family members.

The Groom's Parents are an obvious choice. Does he have brothers or sisters? Are there uncles, aunts or grandparents? It's a chance for you find out more about his family, which again protects you against developing a speech which may offend.

Importantly, by talking to people who have known The Groom since he was young (and in the case of his Mum, very young) it gives you the opportunity to find out more about his childhood.

For my own wedding, my Best Man took the trouble to interview my mother, even though she was overseas at the time!

I'm not saying you should track down every living relative. The law of diminishing returns will kick in! Just identify a handful (maybe only two or three) close family members. Chances are you'll get the bulk of the best insights, provided you pick the right people.

Then and ONLY then do I suggest you move on to…

Conversation 4: The Friends

This is where most Best Men begin their research (if they talk to anyone at all beforehand).

That's a mistake.

Immersing yourself in the Friends' Agenda too early in the speech development process runs the risk of being diverted in some unhelpful directions. You also risk building up that pressure of expectation before your speech development is properly underway.

By waiting until *after* you've spoken to the couple and to the family, it'll be much easier for you to put the friends' agenda into the right context.

Again, remember to use your list of Qualities to help guide the conversation. Introduce a specific Quality and listen to what friends say in response. This will help you 'road test' your Qualities and also provide you with fresh, relevant material.

Top tips for these conversations

Keep a record

- Either paper and pen, or electronic. If people say something surprising, jot it down. If they tell you a story, jot it down. Anything that catches your interest, jot it down.

- Relax about whether what people tell you seems funny or not. If they do make a funny comment, try to capture their exact words. But remember, you're still in intelligence gathering mode.

Stories, stories, stories!

- These are gold for later on.

Get specific

- Encourage people to be as precise as possible: How long ago did X happen? Where were they? What exactly was said? Get the details.

The following is a set of questions I find particularly useful for flushing out some good material:

How would you describe The Groom?

Allow the other person to give their answer and then ask…

How do you know that's true?

In other words, what specific examples can you give me which *show* The Groom in action?

By having chats with the right people and using these tips, you'll quickly build up a stock of raw material about The Groom.

I suggest you crack on with those intelligence gathering activities right away *before* reading the rest of this book.

You'll get so much more from the remaining sections of this book if you've got your raw material in front of you. So, pick up the phone and get chatting. You don't have to meet face-to-face.

Make the call!

As for the chat with yourself, put some music on, go for a run, pump some weights, do whatever it is that you do, and think through what you really want to say about The Groom.

Remember: the clearer the better.

It might only be one word, but it *must* be positive. It must also relate to his qualities as a person, because that's what will connect with your audience.

Have fun and when you're ready, we'll move on to the 2nd Key where we'll start to organise your material...

1st Key - Summary

Avoid a common mistake made by many Best Men which is to launch straight in by writing a script from the beginning.

Instead, start by having a think about what you really want to say about The Groom. Identify his Great Gift and then write it down to give yourself an anchor for your speech.

Next, make a list of all the Qualities (good and bad) which best characterise the Groom.

Only then should you pick up the phone or start sending emails to arrange conversations with:

- The Groom
- The Bride
- The Family
- The Friends

To help ensure you make the most of these conversations, remember to:

- Hunt for stories
- Be specific about the details
- Keep a record

Hit the phone

Simon Bucknall

The 2nd Key

How to organise your material

Well, how did you get on?

- Have you had some conversations?

- Have you gathered some intelligence about The Groom?

- Have you established his Great Gift?

If you haven't done so, then please stop here.

Pick up the phone and **talk** to some people!

You need some raw material in front of you before you can take the next step. Your material doesn't have to be pretty, it doesn't have to be word perfect, but you do need *something* as a start point.

There's little value in reading this section in the abstract. We did agree that this book would work best if it's practical, remember?

If you *have* got some raw material, that's great! We're under way.

Let's take the next step then, which is to organise your raw material by identifying potential Themes for your speech. The key to this is to take a step back from your material and *start to organise it.*

WARNING: *resist the temptation simply to dump your material into your speech document!*

If you plunge into the scripting too soon, you'll lose direction and risk getting tangled up. Often speakers try to prepare their speech by piecing together lots of little bits without taking a step back. This approach very quickly becomes fiddly because it's almost impossible to get your head around the overall look and feel of the speech.

You need to be strategic. Adopt the mindset of a military strategist, not a dumper truck driver!

To achieve this, we need to look for patterns or 'Themes' which emerge from your raw material. These Themes will form the core building blocks of your speech.

The easiest way to identify the potential Themes is by gathering all of your raw material in one place *so you can see it*. This could be on a big sheet of paper or on post-it notes, a flipchart perhaps, a whiteboard or whatever other format works for you. This will include the list of Qualities you drew up, plus all the comments, stories and material gathered in your conversations.

Take a look at what you have and, thinking about The Groom, then ask yourself this question:

• What are the common Themes?

Again, the object of the exercise is to spot patterns. Given what you know now, how would you cluster your material into more manageable chunks?

Don't worry about the actual order and speech structure itself. We'll look at that later. Just focus on clustering your material according to what your bits and pieces have in common.

This may take a bit of time but, combined with your own knowledge of The Groom, you should be able to focus in on up to half a dozen key Themes. These may or may not be the same as some of the Qualities in your original list. It's up to you!

For example, if The Groom is someone who always needs to be the centre of attention, that could be a Theme.

Or perhaps he can be a bit slow on the uptake? That might be a Theme.

Maybe he's simply a bit anal about things?! That could be a Theme...

There's no right or wrong here. Every Groom is different but see if you can get at least four or five potential Themes...

Once you've done that, make a simple list of your Themes.

Have a look at your list and ask yourself: **is there one Theme which is particularly strong and which could sit above the others?**

It's not essential to do this, but you can add a lot of fun and professionalism to your speech if you give it an overarching

'Big Theme', based on a particular aspect of The Groom's life.

Perhaps he's a lawyer. Could your speech take the form of a Trial?

Or maybe he's big on sport. Can you relate all the Themes of the speech back to sport in some way?

Think of yourself as being a bit like a film director deciding on the look and feel of your film.

When developing my own Best Man Speech, I had a list of various Themes I felt I could use: loyalty, The Groom's capacity for (or lack of) languages, his 'classic English' background (in the armed forces, studying classics, public school), his 'salesman' mentality, often getting into trouble at school.

The Groom had also spent much of his career working in the recruitment industry. After some thinking, it dawned on me that recruitment could be my Big Theme linking all the other smaller Themes together. I began to wonder whether the *courtship* process might be portrayed as being a bit like the *recruitment* process, with The Groom as the candidate.

What Big Theme could you use?

Might it be based on his job?

His favourite hobby?

Some other aspect of his life?

You may remember the idea of a courtroom trial mentioned a moment ago.

This idea came from one of my coaching clients whose Groom was indeed a lawyer. He was the sort who rarely got into trouble. A tough target for my client, the Best Man, wouldn't you think?

So, we developed the idea of the Courtroom Trial to add a sense of fun to his 'misdemeanors'. Dastardly crimes such as:

- Not-getting-into-enough-trouble-when-he-was-at-school (unlike the Best Man who was constantly in trouble)

- Consistent-punctuality-throughout-his-life

- Studying-too-hard-at-college

These were all Themes we had identified early on in the speech development process. *Only later* did we realise they could be reframed as 'crimes'. And only after that were we able to identify the best stories to use as evidence for the jury.

Notice how, *first of all*, we had to become clear about the key Themes we wanted to use. This meant we avoided immersing ourselves too much in the nitty-gritty detail too early. We certainly weren't concerning ourselves with humour in the early stages. That came later.

Take some time to reflect on your raw material. See if you can identify some smaller Themes. If you spot a potential Big

Theme, that's a bonus.

Either way, as you'll see very shortly, by establishing a list of Themes, you're taking an important step towards carving out the structure for your speech, which is what we'll cover in the 3rd Key.

2nd Key - Summary

Gather all your raw material in one place.

Cluster the material into as many as six Themes.

A high-potential Theme will likely be a quality, trait or insight which in some way characterises The Groom.

Consider whether there's a single overarching 'Big Theme' which can overlay your entire speech.

Simon Bucknall

The 3rd Key

How to structure your speech

You've gathered your intelligence and you've done some clustering to identify possible Themes. Perhaps you have as few as two or three, or as many as six or more.

Time now to talk about Speech Structure, which is where things really start to take shape. There are a number of ways to do it but, however your speech is structured, simplicity is the key.

I cannot overstate this enough: *your structure has to be simple*. Only with a simple structure will your audience be able to follow you and *only with a simple structure* will you be in a position to stay on track, especially if you want to speak without notes!

More on that in the 7th Key later on.

How do you structure a Best Man Speech?

The simplest way to think about structure is in three parts:

1.   A Beginning

2.   A Middle

3.   An Ending

All well and good but how should you approach each of those three sections?

Let me suggest at this point that you grab a pen and paper and write down the following headings. Relax about how you'll develop each of these elements. We'll deal with them in turn shortly.

At this stage, just get them jotted down and clear in your mind.

BEGINNING

Build Rapport

Establish Direction

MIDDLE

Key Point 1

Key Point 2

Key Point 3

ENDING

Groom's Great Gift

Toast!

What you have here are the core building blocks for a Best Man Speech. Think of them as the 'girders' of your structure. As you can see, they are grouped into three main sections.

In my experience, this is the simplest, most flexible template you can use and it provides a great platform on which to develop your content.

Now for the weird bit.

When preparing your speech, I recommend you work through the sections *in reverse order.*

Your ending

Let's begin with the last (and in many ways the easiest) part of the entire speech: The Toast.

I say 'easy' because it's something you'll definitely do – I hope! Your audience is expecting you to give a Toast and what better way to finish your speech on a high point?

There's more good news here too. You don't have to do anything clever. Just play it safe. The sincerity with which you speak is the important thing.

Here's one example:

"Ladies and gentlemen, will you please be upstanding. Raise your glasses and join me in a toast: To The Bride and Groom."

Done!

Let me emphasise. I'm not saying you should or must say exactly this. I'm just giving an example of how a Toast can be phrased. To be honest, *how* you deliver the Toast in terms of energy and excitement will be every bit as important as the precise words you choose. More on delivery a bit later.

Finishing with a heartfelt Toast is the traditional way to end the speech. You're guaranteed a big round of applause from the audience and you can sit down and feel very good about what you've accomplished.

So, right now, take a moment to scribble down the words for *your* Toast. What will you say? Keep it short and keep it simple.

You might want to say: 'Bride and Groom'. You might say 'Adorable Couple'. Or you might even say 'Mr & Mrs… Boom-duh-di-boom'. *[Though not, of course, if their surname isn't 'Boom-duh-di-boom.' Ed.]*

It's up to you. Go with what you feel sounds right.

Starting with the end in mind is also useful because it focuses you on what you're building towards. The Toast is where you want to end up. You want to finish on a positive note with The Bride and Groom happy and with your audience cheering.

What this means is that immediately before you give The Toast, you'll probably want to say some nice things about The Bride and Groom *as a couple*.

Think about the following questions:

- How do you feel about The Bride and Groom as a couple?

- What do you wish for them in their marriage?

- How has The Groom changed since meeting His Bride (in a positive way!)?

Your answers to these questions will give you a sincere, warm-hearted build-up to The Toast. This means you will end your speech on a real high for the audience.

Once you've got that nailed, we're ready to move back a step in the Speech Structure: to The Groom's Great Gift.

You may remember we talked about this earlier. It's 'What-you-really-want-to-say-about-The-Groom-as-a-man-and-as-a-friend'.

Or in other words…

His single greatest quality.

What I have found, both as a speaker at weddings and as a professional speaker, is that there is tremendous power in single-mindedness.

That's not to say you can't talk about a range of topics in your speech. What I mean is, if you can identify the one quality *above all others* which most distinguishes The Groom (and this needs to be serious) then you have the potential to achieve real impact.

It'll be all the more hard-hitting precisely because it comes **after** the main body of your speech, which will likely contain some light-hearted stories that poke fun.

I know of one very experienced after dinner speaker who makes a point of including something serious towards the end of his speech. Even though much of the rest of the speech is very funny, he finds sincerity and seriousness really add drama and emotional impact to the talk. It also surprises the audience which, done appropriately, is no bad thing. Surprise makes you more memorable.

I found this single-mindedness to be tremendously helpful in developing and delivering my own speech when referencing The Groom's strong sense of loyalty.

It can feel a bit strange, though, focusing on a single idea in this way. When you know someone well (and I assume you *do* know The Groom pretty well!) it can be tempting to highlight a number of positive qualities. Fair enough, but do give some thought to the *number one* quality which stands above all the rest.

This gives cut through and will achieve much greater impact with the audience than simply reeling off a checklist.

Your middle

Now we move back to the Middle part of your speech which, as you may remember, comprises Three Key Points.

One of the great speakers of the American public speaking profession, Bill Gove, was once asked for his top tip on public speaking. He replied:

"Simple. Make a point, tell a story. Or tell a story and then make a point."

Isn't it simple?

Bill Gove mentored many of the speakers who reached the pinnacle of the professional speaking industry in the United States, so his advice is worth taking on board.

The truth is that stories are the 'gold' of your speech, which is why the conversations you had earlier were so important.

In the main body of your speech, the best advice I can offer you is to make Points about The Groom, and then use stories to illustrate them.

If you take a look at your material, you should find you've already made a start on this. Each Theme you've identified is a potential 'Point' you could make about The Groom.

So, which are your strongest three Themes?

For example, if you have The Groom down as someone who's

always *the life and soul of the party*, that might be a Key Point.

Not getting into trouble enough might be a second.

Being forgetful might be a third.

Once you've identified your strongest three Themes (or Points as we'll now call them), have a think about the potential stories you can use to illustrate them.

One, maximum two, stories per Point is plenty.

Beware! Many speakers make the mistake of assuming that a perfectly good, strong story 'Isn't interesting enough' or 'Won't be funny enough'. They then rule out a whole truckload of potentially cracking material.

This explains why so much material in Best Man Speeches is lifted off the internet – because speakers lack faith in the quality of real-life material to be 'funny'. Be assured, if your material is authentic, that's much more important if you really want to serve your audience and do a good job for your friend!

Remember, humour is something you unearth, not insert. Just because the story doesn't *seem* funny at this stage doesn't matter. What *does* matter is that the story be true(ish!) and be related to the Point you're trying to make.

Bonus Tip

If tricky, use this short process, which I find helpful for identifying material for my own speeches.

Remember the questions I suggested you could use during your conversations in the 1st Key? You can use them here too!

First, think about the Point you want to make.

Secondly, ask yourself this question:

How do I know that's true?

In other words, how do you know the Point you're making about The Groom is true? What did you see? What happened? What did he say or do? What was the result?

Something must have happened in the past for you to come up with the Point in the first place. Your job is to figure out what that event was: a conversation, an incident or an encounter of some other kind?

If you find it difficult to answer that question, it's not because the evidence doesn't exist. It's because you haven't yet unearthed it in your own head or the heads of others. You may even find it useful to go back to some of the people you've previously spoken with. Only now, you've got much greater clarity of purpose. You're more like a journalist, seeking further detail.

We'll cover the storytelling skills themselves in more detail later, so don't worry about crafting your stories to perfection at this stage. All you're looking to do right now is to identify your three strongest Key Points and then link them to relevant supporting material drawn from The Groom's life experience and/or what you or others have observed.

Your beginning

Finally, we come to the Beginning of your speech, which is where many Best Men make the mistake of *starting* the speech development process.

If you've been following me so far, by the time you reach this point in the journey, you should already have a rough outline of what your speech will contain.

Doesn't that make your beginning much, much easier to construct?

There are two elements to consider here:

• Build Rapport

• Establish Direction

As before, we'll take them in *reverse order*.

First, **Establish Direction**.

This is important because your audience needs to know where they're going or, to be more precise, where you'll be taking them.

To establish direction, all you need do is briefly summarise what you'll be covering in the Middle section of your speech. Simple!

What you say here will depend, of course, on what you'll be using as your Three Key Points. If you have an overarching Big Theme, this is also where you would introduce it so that people can tune in.

Here's an example of how this played out in my own Best Man speech:

[2:15 mins]

"Now Will, as many of you will know, works in recruitment.

And very successful he is too.

And having worked in the industry myself, what I'm always struck by is the similarity between the recruitment game and the courtship game.

Many may enter the race but there's only one job in the end...

So first, bearing in mind the rigorous selection process William had to progress through in order to win Hannah's hand in marriage...

First, consider the application form..."

Think of it as setting up the rest of your speech.

All I'm trying to do at the beginning is to tee the audience up, without giving the game away. My intention as a speaker is to ensure they have some idea of where I'll be taking them so they can enjoy the ride.

How will you set up *your* speech so that *your* audience has an idea of where you'll be taking them? And what could you say to whet their appetite so that they enjoy the ride?

Once you've drafted that, you're ready to move onto 'what-you-say-right-at-the-very-start' of your speech: **Building Rapport**.

Some tips upfront here.

Avoid classic clangers when it comes to openings:

"Can you hear me at the back...?"

"Erm... so I don't give speeches very often so..."

"Erm..."

"Erm...hello. How are you all doing? You're OK? Great..."

You might think these openings endear you to the audience. But at the very least, *under no circumstances apologise for yourself in front of the audience.*

All this does is devalue you and your speech in the eyes of the audience by suggesting you don't really know what you're doing. If you went to a restaurant and the waiter apologised for the fact that they don't have a very good chef in today, how would you feel as a diner?

The same is true with audiences. No-one wants to listen to a speaker with no faith in his own ability to be of value. Your willingness to commit to your material is vital, which is why it's so important for the speech content to be your own.

So, how should you start?

Building rapport is all about finding common ground.

Find some things that you and the audience have in common and then talk about them.

There are a million and one ways in which you can do this and you might even find that something happens on the day itself which you can then reference!

Classic examples include the location of the wedding, your experience of the service, the singing, the dinner itself or perhaps an idea you'll be using in your speech.

In my own speech, I opened as follows:

"Ladies and Gentlemen, you know sometimes, you just get that feeling, that you've got two people destined to get along with one another…"

If you listen to the video carefully, those were my very first words. The reason I used them was because I felt confident most people in the room *could* agree with the idea that sometimes you *do* just get that feeling about two people being destined to get along with one another! All I'm looking to do is find common ground with the audience, even if it's just a brief remark.

Traditionally, people who were invited to a wedding, but couldn't make it, would send a telegram with a message of support for the couple. Nowadays, they're more likely to send an email or a card.

Check with The Groom whether there are any messages for you to read out. They're a great way to build rapport early in your speech. They also have the advantage of being a very *safe* way, especially if you are feeling anxious about the speech. We'll look at how to handle nerves later on.

What you have in common with the audience here is a shared interest in the people who wanted to be there, but couldn't.

So, your opening might run something like:

"Ladies and Gentlemen, a very warm welcome on this special day.

As you may know, it's customary for the Best Man to read telegrams from those who would like to be here, but couldn't make it.

So, let me first read to you what Bill and Sarah have written…
X, Y and Z would have loved to attend but send their very best
wishes…etc. etc."

You're on safe ground. You're fulfilling your duties as a Best Man. You can also read the messages rather than having to memorise them, so there's little chance of making a mistake.

You do of course also have the option of inventing some 'telegrams' of your own, *if* you feel it appropriate!

Now, that could be fun…

Stand-up comedians are EXPERTS at building rapport. They have to be because they never know who is in their audience and it's usually a very broad range of people. Good comedians understand the key to making humour work: the audience has to be relaxed (not tense) and for that to happen, you *must have rapport* with them. Apologising for yourself is so damaging because, if anything, it introduces unnecessary tension.

Remember, there are all kinds of ways you could break the ice. You can reference the day you've had so far, how enjoyable the service was, the weather, where you are in the country. You could even reference something mentioned by one of the other speakers.

This allows the audience to get to know you a bit, before you set some direction and move into the main body of your speech.

Think of it as the beginning of a chat in the pub rather than the opening to a speech. A conversational feel is what you should aim for. Do that and they'll warm to you right away. Your audience wants you to do well. It's in their interest!

In the next Key, we'll look at ways you can develop your content.

3rd Key - Summary

Structuring your speech is an absolutely critical step in the Best Man Speech development process.

- Keep your structure simple

- In your Beginning, **Build Rapport** and **Establish Direction**

- In your Middle, make **Three Key Points** and use stories to illustrate

- In your Ending, elaborate on **The Groom's Great Gift,** say positive things about The Bride and Groom, then **Toast!**

Work your way backwards through your speech because, at first, crafting a Toast is much easier than crafting a 'blind opening'.

Remember that your Three Points will emerge from the Themes you identified in Key 2.

Bill Gove's top tip for communication is to make a point, tell a story.

To build rapport, find common ground with the audience, not just with a few of your mates in the back corner!

Avoid diluting your impact by apologising upfront. Reading the 'telegrams' can be a useful, safe way to open your speech.

🔑 The 4th Key

How to develop your content

You should now have a rough overall structure for your speech.

It absolutely does not have to be word perfect. You might not even have a script. What you should have is an overall flow with the core building blocks in place.

Let's now look at how you can develop this content, and the stories in particular, so you can take your speech to the next level.

A common mistake Best Men make is to assume that they have to stick with their first draft. In other words, they are given some material and then plop it 'unedited' into the speech. This is a bit like the gardener who plants flowers and then never takes the time to water or prune them.

Ask any comedian and they'll tell you that jokes take work. They have to be nurtured. What starts out as mediocre, with the right handling, can become very powerful material. But it does take some effort! Needless to say, The Weak Man Speaker finds it easier just to leave the material in its raw form, which is a shame.

Step 1 - Create a draft script

If you possibly can, I encourage you to write out a full draft for your speech. Alternatively, record yourself on your phone talking about the speech off-the-cuff and then *write that down* as a transcript.

Relax about whether it sounds perfect or not. At this stage it's important that your draft *doesn't* sound perfect. What matters is that you capture the gist of what you want to say.

Darren LaCroix, 2001 World Champion of Public Speaking, makes a neat observation about this:

"Great speeches aren't written; they're re-written."

Food for thought, eh? Only once you have a draft script to work with can you edit effectively. If the speech is merely in your head, you'll find it very hard to develop a compelling speech. Certainly, it'll be difficult to do successive rounds of editing!

What most people do is write the speech out in paragraphs.

Don't.

Why?

Because take it from me, memorising paragraphs is a nightmare!

Write one sentence per line. It's so much easier to edit that way. One sentence per line also forces you to keep your sentences short and helps you to internalise later on.

Step 2 - Edit

Once you have a script, go through it line by line and cut out as many words as you can. The fewer words you use the better, so long as you communicate everything you need to get across.

If you spot any phrases such as 'Well, having said that'…'Of course'…'Something else which I'd really like to say is…'

Cut!

You want as tight a draft as possible, even if on the day itself you embellish and reintroduce those conversational fillers. I receive dozens of eCritiques from Best Men each year, asking for feedback on their scripts. The most common issue, text-wise, is the use of unnecessary filler phrases.

They may read well on the page but when spoken out loud, they just sound clumsy. Read your script aloud and you'll find it much easier to judge whether you really need all those long sentences…

Step 3 - Develop your stories

Now let's look at developing your core material: your stories.

I have three tips for you. They're very simple, practical and, most of all, they work. I say this because I've developed them through working with countless individuals on their speech development, including not only Best Men but also people in a wide range of professions.

Tip 1 - Give Brief Context

Ask yourself:

- How long ago did the events of the story take place?

- Where did they happen?

- Who was there?

Aim to be as specific as possible with these details but *without going on for too long*. Just enough for people to 'get it', so their heads are in the right place. Three or four descriptors should be enough to give you context.

You don't need a lot of detail, but the quality of the detail you use is important.

Here's an example from one of my corporate speeches.

"May 2001. Central London. Leaving drinks from my first job. And I'm having a panic…"

Do you see how quickly it's possible to set context?

In my Best Man Speech, there's a good example of setting context when introducing a story about The Groom doing telesales.

[6:00 mins]

"He gave some examples…a wealth of relevant experience!

Take for example the time when he was temping for a telesales agency…

Flogging photocopiers to small businesses… [brief pause]

In Dusseldorf."

Notice how specific I had to be with the details to get the audience's minds where I wanted them to be.

And if you haven't watched the YouTube clip, notice the importance of the word 'Dusseldorf'. The detail not only adds impact but also humour (more on that later).

Tip 2 - Identify a Critical Moment

For any story to have impact, something has to happen at some point! The Critical Moment in a story is the point at which things change. In other words, the outcome of the story is determined.

The best storytellers are very good at identifying the Critical Moments in a story and dramatising them for the listener.

Take a look at one of *your* stories and have a think:

- What does that story 'say' about The Groom?

- What's the most critically important moment which determined the outcome of the story?

- Was it something The Groom said? If so, his exact words could have terrific impact. Was it something he did or how he reacted? Or was it something done by somebody else?

Be as specific as you can about the *exact* circumstances in which the activity or incident took place because that's the crux of the drama.

Think of slow motion in films. Which 'moment' in your story would you convert to slow motion if you could? Your answer to that question should give you some clues to when the Critical Moment takes place.

The temptation when telling stories is to gloss over the specifics, especially if it's an experience you yourself have had. That's because we take for granted the fact that we were there, struggling to convey the drama to someone who wasn't.

This explains why so often, at the end of a story, you hear the line:

"Well, I guess you had to be there…"

All rather embarrassing.

The real power of identifying a Critical Moment is that it enables you to bring that moment to life for the audience. This creates drama and *truly transforms* the impact of the story on the audience. You'll also find that the story is more likely to become humorous.

As you saw a few moments ago, The Groom I spoke about had experience in telesales. From speaking to him and to friends, I knew he had done some pretty tough jobs when working in that industry.

With the Dusseldorf story, it would have been very easy to say something like:

"So, he spent day after day calling businesses in Dusseldorf, talking to them in English and hanging up if he couldn't make himself understood."

True but not terribly imaginative. Notice how there's no drama. There's no Critical Moment.

My challenge as a speaker was to recreate a Critical Moment by bringing to life Will's explanation of his role to Hannah who, remember, is supposedly 'interviewing' him for the job of spouse.

Let's pick up from where we left off at [6:15 mins].

"… flogging photocopiers to small businesses…[brief pause]

In Dusseldorf.

Again, Hannah was impressed!

'I didn't know you spoke German!'

'I don't.'

'So how did you communicate?'

'I asked them if they spoke English.'

'And if they didn't, you...'

'Put the phone down.'"

Do you see the difference between the two versions?

Identify the Critical Moments in your stories and really bring them to life. In the drama of The Moment lies enjoyment for your audience.

To do this does take emotional commitment. You *must commit* to the power of that moment, because if you don't, your audience is much less likely to be with you.

Tip 3 - Use Dialogue

Such a simple tip but a hugely effective one!

If characters are speaking in your stories, use dialogue. Play back to your audience the exact words people used. It's so much more engaging, even if it's not intended to be a funny line.

Dialogue, dialogue, dialogue.

Hamlet may have been pondering whether or not to commit suicide.

What he actually said was:

"To be or not to be."

Priceless.

The precise words a character uses in any of your stories make a *huge* difference to your impact. Again, notice in the above example of Dusseldorf how it's all about the dialogue. That's what brings the Critical Moment to life.

Here's another example.

[5:10 mins]

"Keen as ever to make a good first impression, Will opted for the suave sophisticated approach...

'Hey babe! Take a look at my big ones!'"

The 'Hey babe!' line was never going to be hilarious. But if you watch the clip, you'll see how the dialogue makes it that bit more entertaining for the audience.

Use dialogue and really let yourself go because when you adopt the voices of others, we hear *the voice of the character*, rather than *you*! It's a really effective way of adding variety, energy and drama to your speech.

4th Key - Summary

- Write a draft script

- One sentence per line

- Edit line by line

- Give brief context to open your stories

- Identify and dramatise your Critical Moments

- Use dialogue

Develop and hone

If you're serious about crafting your speech, you may want to consider our eCritique service, as part of my coaching offer.

You email your script to me and I'll go through it line by line and send it back with comments and suggestions.

To find out more, just visit our website:

www.theartofconnection.co.uk

Visit the coaching section for details or you can email us:

info@theartofconnection.co.uk

Simon Bucknall

The 5th Key

How to find humour

Entire books have been written on humour. It's a huge subject. It's also very subjective. What one person finds hilarious leaves another person cold.

By now you should have your structure and key chunks of content in place. What you'll get from this Key are some techniques used by humorous speakers and comedians to help uncover humour which is hiding within material you *already* have.

What often happens is that Best Men insert a joke. Usually, it's one taken from the internet. The problem with this is that the joke lacks authenticity. The audience will usually spot it's not your gag. To be honest, it's a bit rubbish.

Keep faith with the material you have. This material is more authentic and, as a result, infinitely more rewarding for you and for the audience.

And if they don't laugh?

Well, what's the worst that can happen?

You give a sincere, heartfelt speech which people appreciate and which is guaranteed to delight The Parents of The Bride.

But to give yourself the best chance of laughs, consider any or all of the following ideas...

Technique 1 - Setup-Punch

Catching an audience by surprise is a great way to trigger laughter. Lead them in a certain direction and then hit them with something they're not expecting. Very often, the bigger the surprise, the bigger the laugh you get.

That's what the setup-punch structure is all about in comedy. It's the basis of a huge percentage of funny lines. Lead the audience to expect one thing... then say/do the opposite.

But to surprise them, *you have to commit to the punchline!*

Commit to the punchline

Again, this is a common issue with the scripts I critique – potentially funny material is buried in the middle of a paragraph with no evidence of the speaker's willingness to really highlight the punchline for the benefit of the audience.

How do you 'commit' to a punchline?

Well, the first step is to identify precisely which phrase(s) or word(s) are most likely to make the audience react.

Secondly, consider a short pause immediately before you deliver that word or phrase. Even if only very short, the pause helps trigger a sense of anticipation on the part of the audience.

Thirdly, take a close look at your tone of voice when delivering the punchline. If it's a sarcastic line, then your voice should reflect that; if whimsical, then inflect that.

In the spirit of authenticity, there's an example in my own speech.

[3:35 mins]

"I invite you to consider the possibility that the man you thought you knew is but a myth. An illusion. A conjurer. A master in the art of concealment!

Qualities of good taste, discretion and irreproachable manners…[short pause]

Concealed by this man for years."

Notice how, in the live version, I really 'hit' that final line for greater impact. Listen to the recording and then try reading the above excerpt out loud yourself, but at an even pace and in a monotone. You should notice a difference!

Here's another example at [6:45mins].

"And there's more!

Because buried deep within this man is an unbridled passion, energy, drive and thirst, appetite for hard work...[short pause]

Artfully concealed."

Again, the pause and inflection in my voice was quite deliberate – and important.

Think about how you might surprise *your* audience in *your* speech. What could you lead them to expect and then spring on them?

One simple way to achieve this is to look at the observations you're making about The Groom and then invert them. Say the opposite of what you mean. The sense of contrast you create opens up the possibility of humour, which in its simplest form explains the impact of sarcasm and irony.

If The Groom is XYZ, why not suggest the precise opposite? Your audience will soon cotton on to the fact that you're not being entirely serious.

So if The Groom is always late, then commend him for being on time... and provide appropriate examples! Tongue-in-cheek humour like this may seem rather simple and obvious, but with audience members who just want to enjoy themselves, it can be remarkably effective.

Another way to uncover setup-punch opportunities in your speech is through using the Rule Of Three.

You simply list three things. The first two are the setup. The third is the punch. The good news is that you can use this technique almost anywhere in your speech.

For example, the three GREAT loves of The Groom's life: travel... fine wine... bee-keeping.

(NOTE: check beforehand that The Bride and Parents are not keen bee-keepers!)

A good example of the use of the Rule Of Three comes later in my speech when recounting the story of The Groom's encounter with a frozen food salesmen on his front doorstep.

[8:00mins]

"Consider the dilemma, ladies and gentlemen.

On the one hand, a treacherous two minute walk to the local shops to buy food, fraught with danger...

And on the other hand, thirty six chicken kievs at £50 a pop.

Ladies and gentlemen, when this man is in the kitchen, it's Chicken Tonight!

And tomorrow night...

And the night after that..."

Technique 2 - Use toppers

This is simply a comment you make on something you have just said (or that has just happened).

Think of it as the comedian's equivalent of a witty aside, which you add 'ON TOP' of what's been said.

Above, you can see the *'It's Chicken Tonight!* [pause] *and Tomorrow Night...'* line.

This is not only a Rule Of Three, it was also a Topper but I didn't come up with that in one go. It only occurred to me as I reflected on the idea of The Groom being too lazy to go shopping, instead opting for the frozen chicken door-to-door salesman.

Then I made the link with the advert and consumer brand 'Chicken Tonight'. It wasn't until a day or two before the wedding that it occurred to me that with thirty plus chicken kievs in his freezer, it'd be chicken pretty much every night!

Here's another example of a Topper, right at the start of the speech. This one wasn't even scripted! It just seemed like the right thing to say at the time.

[0:10 mins]

"And I can still remember the night when Will first told me about Hannah.

He said, 'Guess what? I've met someone!'

Well, that's a good start."

I should add that while I found the Topper here faintly amusing, I never expected it to prompt as much laughter as it did. Proof, if any were needed, that your audience will be the true judge of your humour, not you!

Again, comedians are experts in the use of the Topper technique. Check out Rhod Gilbert for a particularly good example in his 'Lost Luggage' sketch.

If you search on YouTube for: 'Rhod Gilbert luggage' you should find it easily enough.

Classic!

Imagine how long it would have taken him to build up, test and then hone that routine.

If you've seen the film *Four Weddings and a Funeral*, you may remember Hugh Grant's character giving a Best Man Speech right at the beginning of the film.

He says:

"Anyway, my job today is to talk about Angus…and there are no skeletons in his closet…

Or so I thought!"

Again, great Topper.

They're so simple to use and you'll find there are opportunities right the way through your speech, especially if you combine it with the technique of looking for setup-punch surprises.

The trick with this is to adopt the right mindset. The best Toppers are often a form of 'critical commentary' or afterthought, as if added by someone else. Think of it as being a bit like sitting on the sofa watching TV and then shouting at the television!

Your job is to adopt that 'armchair commentator' approach to your own speech…

Try reading the script out loud and then imagine yourself listening to it on the radio. What comments would you make?

You may find Toppers particularly useful early on where you're establishing the direction of your speech for the audience.

One Best Man client of mine had an opening which we improved through the use of a Topper.

The original version went something like this:

"So, in asking me to be his Best Man, Pete knew it was because I would never dream of saying anything bad about him."

Have a think for a moment. What Toppers could you use here?

How about...

"So, in asking me to be his Best Man, Pete knew it was because I would never dream of saying anything bad about him.

Or so he thought."

A simple addition. In the cold of light of day, perhaps not obviously funny. But in the context of a wedding audience, guaranteed to provoke a response.

Do you see how this can work?

It's not all about bellyaching laughs.

Get some small chuckles in early and you're more likely to

relax the audience and secure even bigger laughs later on.

Let me give you one more example, which builds on the opening of my own speech. For clarity, I've labelled the Punchline and Topper in [square brackets]. Equally, you may find it easier simply to view on YouTube.

[0:10 mins]

"And I can still remember the night when Will first told me about Hannah.

He said, 'Guess what? I've met someone!'

Well, that's a good start. [Pause for laughter]

He said, 'Her name's Hannah and I'm very excited about her.'

Naturally, as a friend of his, I was intrigued. 'What's she like? [brief pause] How will she cope... with this man? And are they well suited?'

[PUNCHLINE] Imagine my relief when I learnt that Hannah is a specialist...in working with difficult children.

[pause]

[TOPPER] That's right, right from the start I knew they were destined to get along just fine..."

Again, that last Topper was not something I'd planned. It just felt like the right thing to say, given the way the audience reacted.

What I'm saying is that you should feel good about going with the flow during your speech. Think of it as a conversation, and when audience members laugh or react in any way to what you say or do, they're 'talking to you'.

Go with that. Run with it. When you comment on that reaction, you'll not only be using Toppers which will make your material more entertaining, you'll also be more spontaneous and natural, which is *wonderful* for the audience.

Good, eh?

Technique 3 - The callback

What's a callback?

Think of it as an 'in-joke' between you and the audience.

It's when you 'callback' to (or refer back to) something which has already been said or already happened *some time earlier.*

This is a hugely effective technique which I first remember encountering when learning from Craig Valentine, 1999 World Champion of Public Speaking, an outstanding speaker and a great teacher.

A callback refers back to something that took place a few minutes, hours, days, months or even years earlier. Think of good friends of yours. When you meet, chances are you talk about and banter over events which may have happened years ago!

Many nicknames are a form of callback.

To work well in a Best Man Speech, a callback MUST be something which you *and* the vast majority of the audience can relate to.

It might be something that took place on the wedding day itself; or perhaps it's something which one of the other speakers has said; it might even be something you referred to earlier in your own speech.

But there's no point trying to callback to something which half the people in the room haven't experienced.

In my own speech, I created my own callback by telling the audience about the Ushers' Challenge.

[1:30 mins]

"I should say that Rich and I have both been presented with a challenge in these two speeches.

At the start of the meal today, we were presented with five random words selected by the ushers.

Which we're required to insert into our speeches without the audience noticing.

So I would invite you to look out during the course of what follows for those five words.

I obviously shan't tell you where they come. It'll be up to you to spot them.

But just to give you a hint in the right direction, the words are: crocodile... semi-naked... moist... beaver and anti-disestablishmentarianism."

You can tell by my use of language that I was pretty much having to do this off-the-cuff.

If you watch and listen to the YouTube video, you'll hear me stumble over *'which we w-were required to...'* As for the phrase: *'give you a hint in the right direction...'* I'm not quite sure where I was going with the syntax on that one!

Anyway, back to callbacks.

Notice at this point, there's no callback yet because the audience weren't there when the ushers set the challenge for Richard and me (although we're all at the meal together, so they can relate to it easily enough).

The actual callback comes six and a half minutes later in the speech, when at [7:21mins] this happens:

"As luck would have it, the phone...the doorbell rang.

And who do you think should be standing there on the doorstep?

A semi-naked, cross-breed crocodile-beaver, of anti-disestablishment views, moist because it was raining!"

Do you see?

Now it's a callback.

Comedian Eddie Izzard is an absolute master of this technique. He sows all kinds of seeds early in his routines, which he later 'calls back' to.

Just watch one of his shows for some great examples, especially 'Dressed To Kill' or 'Definite Article'. Well worth checking out.

You may also find a particular line or phrase you can use repeatedly during the course of your speech.

A bit like a chorus, which functions just like a callback.

Do you remember the Best Man who decided to put his lawyer Groom on trial? After each of the three Charges, he delivered the following line:

"Ladies and Gentlemen, members of the Jury, you have heard all the evidence. Do you find the defendant innocent or guilty?

'Guilty as charged!'"

That was the line.

The first time he delivered that refrain, it was amusing for the audience.

But the second time, the audience started to catch on *because they'd heard the line before*. It's a form of callback.

By the *third* time, the audience absolutely knew what was coming.

And they all joined in:

"Guilty as charged!"

Perhaps there's a way you can build a callback of this kind into your speech? A bit like a chorus line?

If so, get really clear on the exact words and use them repeatedly during the speech. Think of it being like the chorus in a song.

5th Key - Summary

When you surprise an audience with something unexpected, you stand a much better chance of making them laugh.

Avoid the trap of assuming that you have to make the audience laugh within the first five seconds. Faint amusement in the form of a few chuckles early on is a good start. By breaking the ice in this way, you gain momentum and give humorous moments that come later in the speech a better chance of success.

Three tried and tested techniques which can help you to unearth humour in your speech include:

- Setup-Punch (including Rule Of Three)

- The Topper

- The Callback

You should find that by using them, you stay true to yourself without having the pressure of having to insert gags off the internet.

Be assured, authentic humour will beat synthetic gags nicked from elsewhere *every time*.

If you try to tell a joke and it falls flat, you're in trouble.

If by being authentic and using your own material, you don't get the reaction you hoped for, you'll find it much, much easier to carry on as if nothing has happened.

Simon Bucknall

The 6th Key

How to handle nervousness

Interesting, isn't it?

So often, we talk about 'feeling nervous', terrified even. If this sounds like you, then be assured you're in good company!

You see, back in May 2001, I was leaving my first job. Forty colleagues came to wish me well. Some even brought me a farewell gift.

Nice.

What I wasn't expecting was to have to give a speech. When someone called out *'Speech!'* I knew I was in trouble. Felt a bit like being the guilty party at a police line-up, not that I've *had* that experience.

Do any of the following symptoms sound familiar?

My hands started shaking. My face went red. Worst of all, I stopped breathing properly because when I get anxious, I only breathe *in*.

Now if you try that (which I suggest you don't) you'll find one of two things will happen: either you'll hyperventilate or pass out.

There I am, standing in front of my colleagues, bent over a desk, panting... through sheer nervousness.

The result? I made a decision to improve. I joined a public speaking club and six years later stood on the stage in Washington DC representing my country in the finals of the

World Championship of Public Speaking.

Along the way, I picked up some useful tips that made a difference for me. Perhaps they'll make a difference for you too.

All of these techniques and insights are drawn from first-hand experience. This is not theory; these are tips and insights which *work*.

Tip 1 - Think 'adrenaline' not 'nerves'

Imagine your dream pin-up.

That's right, your absolute heart-throb. The most gorgeous person you can possibly dream of. Now imagine they enter the room, walk up to you and start chatting.

Is it possible you might flush? Is it possible your heart might race? Is it possible that your breathing might speed a little and go a little shallow?

Danger of Nerves

What you'd be experiencing are the effects of adrenaline coursing through your system. It's the human body's way of saying: *'Get ready. This is going to be big!'*

At school and university, I was really into rugby and athletics. Same thing happened. Usually it was right before the whistle for kick-off or the gun to start the race. My heart would pound, my nerves jangle, butterflies in the stomach and the rest.

It's the same with public speaking. We experience adrenaline but, too often, our minds *interpret* that as 'nervousness'.

Give yourself permission to feel however you feel. You're allowed to experience adrenaline! It's a perfectly natural and human response to a challenging situation.

Notice how this creates a distinction between what you physically experience and *how you interpret that experience*. They are two quite different things.

People often ask me:

"So Simon, you do all this speaking to audiences, week in week out. Do you still get nervous?"

To which my reply is usually:

"In a way… but I don't call the experience 'nerves'. I call it adrenaline."

No, I'm not suggesting you imagine the audience naked… or picture them as rows of cabbages. Faking out your nerves is not, in my experience, terribly helpful.

Too many Best Men worry *about* feeling nervous. Turn this on its head. Allow yourself to harness the adrenaline. It's there to help, not be a hindrance.

Remember, how *you* feel is not the same as how *the audience* feels...

Tip 2 - Remember the audience doesn't care how nervous you are!

That's right!

Your audience doesn't care how nervous you feel, unless you tell them! If you talk about how nervous you're feeling, you'll detract from the value of your speech and risk sowing doubt in the minds of your audience members.

In reality, *they don't care how nervous you are!*

So why tell them?

This really struck me at my leaving drinks from my first job. When I went round afterwards apologising to people for feeling nervous, they said:

"Hey, doesn't matter!"

"Thought it was quite sweet actually. Shows that you'll miss us."

"Really? You were nervous? Didn't even realise."

On the day of the wedding, perhaps more than any other day, your audience *wants you to do well*. They have a vested interest, after all.

Even if you do experience severe adrenaline, just because *you* know about it, doesn't mean *the audience* does!

When I work with groups on this, I always invite people to the front to practice their speaking in front of the audience. When they've finished, I invite them to comment on the experience.

So often, they say:

"Oh, it was terrible! My face went red...my hands were trembling...heart was going DUFF DUFF DUFF..."

I reassure them that that's perfectly natural and OK. Smiling, I then turn to the audience:

"What did you notice?"

CUE: "We couldn't tell! Didn't notice a thing!"

Without exception, the audience's perception is nothing like what the speaker had imagined. Most of the time, the audience doesn't even realise! Think about it: how hard would your heart have to pound for other people to notice, assuming they don't have a stethoscope?

Even if they DO notice, they don't care, frankly! What they

care about is that you do well by entertaining them, by being thought-provoking and by being a good friend.

Tip 3 - Tip chin to chest

Breathlessness was my biggest challenge when the adrenaline kicked in. At my leaving drinks, I was literally unable to breathe properly. Seriously!

Truth is, most of us have a pet nightmare symptom.

To this day, immediately before I go up to speak, I make time to take some slow, deep breaths.

Here's the crucial point.

As you take the breath, tip your chin down, right into your Adam's Apple. Physiologically, this straightens you up and opens your airway, forcing you to breathe deep down using your diaphragm, rather than high up in your chest.

Try it now…

Place one hand just above your waist…

Tip your chin down…

Breathe in…

You should feel your hand move outwards slightly as your diaphragm drops to allow air deep into the lungs.

NOTE: This may feel strange. It might even feel like you're not really taking a proper breath. One of the ironies of breathing is that a shallow breath high up in the chest may *feel like a big breath* but is not a big breath at all!

By using your diaphragm in the way outlined above, you gain two benefits.

First, you provide a solid platform for your voice.

Secondly, you help to settle the adrenaline in your midriff (which is why we get 'butterflies') allowing you to focus more clearly on the job in hand.

Tip 4 - Use your neutral stance

While I'm not a great advocate of artificial, staged movements in public speaking, your physical body can give off powerful signals to an audience.

When the adrenaline kicks in, especially if a speaker interprets this as nervousness, all sorts of little tics can appear.

Whether it's arms folded, the awkward shuffle, legs crossed, lint-picking, the itchy nose... These little things can greatly detract from your impact.

Given the way our minds work, this physical state of anxiety can affect us mentally and emotionally too.

No matter how good your material, if you stare down, with shoulders slumped, hands in pockets and fidget, you're unlikely to make a positive impression on the audience.

This may make you feel more comfortable but remember, it's not about you. It's about The Parents and the audience!

What can you do to project confidence, even if you don't feel it?

The answer is to identify your 'Neutral Stance'. Think of it as like neutral gear in a car: not very exciting, but essential if you're to run through the gears smoothly.

As a Best Man, your Neutral Stance can be your best friend because it guarantees you project confidence, *even if you don't feel confident.*

It does, though, take some conscious effort. That's because a Neutral Stance can feel weird at first. However, what feels weird to you may look entirely comfortable and confident to an audience!

The best way for you to understand the Neutral Stance is for you to experience it. So, if you're sitting down, stand up (unless you're in the car...or the bath).

Make sure you've emptied all your pockets. That means no coins or keys please! No clicky-clicky pens, no sheets of paper.

Just let your hands drop down to your sides and let them hang there. If, while doing this, you're still reading then I'm impressed!

I appreciate that with your hands dropping down by your sides you may feel like a gorilla, but that's OK. Promise.

Most people I've worked with say 'weird'. Some *hate* it. AAAGH! Does it feel like you want to do something with your hands?

Trust me. It may feel weird but to an audience, it looks much better than it does to you.

So why use it?

Answer, because Neutral Stance forces you to strip out all the distractions, freeing you up to speak and move in a natural way.

Am I suggesting you stand like a statue to deliver your speech?

Of course not.

What I am saying is that this can be your default setting. Your neutral gear. Your safe haven if you like. It's like an anchor point, a stance you can dip into when necessary.

Try folding your hands in front of you, just above your waist.

You may feel a bit like a vicar (especially if you are a vicar in real life) but, in fact, this can also work as a Neutral Stance.

It's important not to do the hand wringing, as if you're a dodgy second-hand car dealer, or the white-knuckles-look as if you're on a rollercoaster.

Hold your right hand out, palm facing up as if to say *'Give me five!'* Then drop your left hand into your right and bring both hands into your waist, just above the beltline.

Nice and comfortable; nice and neutral.

These are a couple of options.

You may want to check this out in the mirror or with a friend who can give feedback on what looks right for you.

The key is to decide on your Neutral Stance and then to use it.

Tip 5 - Drink something sweet

Dry mouth can be a big problem for many speakers.

When I ask them what they do about it, 99% of the time they reply:

"Have a drink of water…"

This may surprise you, but a glass of water doesn't help. You need something sweet because it's much better for stimulating the salivary glands.

Water gives the illusion of dealing with dry mouth but it's far better to have a sweet decaf coffee or some fruit juice.

Alcohol may be tempting but I encourage you to avoid it as a way of dealing with nerves.

You'll keep a clearer head and do a better job if you stay off the booze until after your speech. *Then* you can celebrate!

Tip 6 - Practice out loud and turn up the volume

A while back, I did some coaching for one of my neighbours who had a Best Man Speech to deliver.

Brilliant electrician; very quiet speaker.

In my living room, while he read his speech to me out loud, I encouraged him to raise the volume.

More and more and more until he stopped and cried out:

"Feels like I'm shouting!"

"Well, yes!" I said. *"But for me, you're just about the right volume now. Before it was too quiet. Carry on at that level."*

After a couple more minutes, he stopped again:

"You know, it's strange but I feel different just by speaking more loudly. I feel…almost…stronger."

There you go!

That's because by raising the volume you raise the level of vibrations in your physical body. This energises you and affects your state of mind. This is all good when you're wanting to achieve impact in front of an audience.

Have you ever listened to a recording of your own voice?

Is it just me or do you also find it HORRIFIC?

At least, that's what most people say when they hear themselves. AAARGH!

The reason is that how we sound to other people is not how we sound to ourselves.

And *that's* because we hear our own voices through our heads, whereas other people hear us through the *air*. Not only does this affect how it sounds in terms of pitch and accent, it also affects *volume*.

We sound louder to ourselves than we do to others, which is why so often speakers speak too quietly. And that's not great in terms of energy and engagement with the audience.

If you practice your speech out loud (and I strongly encourage you to) even if you start by simply reading out your script, raise your volume until it's uncomfortably loud to you.

As soon as you feel it's too loud, you're about the right volume.

After a while, you should also feel the difference in your physical body. By speaking more loudly, your body (and your head in particular) will vibrate more forcefully.

Weird at first, but very quickly you should find it starts to feel energising. The sound should fill your head!

6th Key - Summary

Some tips for handling nerves and, most importantly, for projecting confidence to the audience.

- Give yourself permission. Remember adrenaline, not nerves

- Chin to Chest, breathe deeply

- Use your Neutral Stance

- Sweet drink on stand-by

- Speak up - be a man not a mouse!

Above all else, remember, it's your friend's wedding day!

So give it some...

Simon Bucknall

The 7th Key

How to handle the practicalities

We're into the home straight. If you've made it this far then I salute you for your effort and commitment!

We've looked at a wide range of techniques, tips and insights to help you develop as a speaker so you can deliver the best possible Best Man Speech for the wedding.

You have a stack of raw material.

You have some core Themes.

You have a simple speech structure into which you've inserted your Themes in the form of three Key Points.

Each of those Key Points is backed up by a simple story or two.

We've looked at how to hone those stories, bringing to life the Critical Moments wherever possible. We've also looked at how to uncover some humour using Setup-Punch, Toppers and Callbacks.

Believe me, by accomplishing all this, your speech will be *light years ahead* of the vast majority of Best Man Speeches.

What's more, you can take these techniques and use them to help you be a better speaker in other aspects of your life, not just at weddings.

So, in this final key, let's take a look at some practicalities, including:

- Using Notes

- How to Practice

- Staging and Mechanics

Using Notes

If you possibly can, deliver your speech without notes.

It may seem terrifying, but believe me, your connection with the audience will be SO much stronger as a result. Your audience will also really appreciate it.

They'll have the sense that you're actually *talking* to them rather than *reading* to them. You may remember we talked before about the advantages of thinking of your speech as a conversation, rather than as a set-piece presentation.

If you decide you DO want to have notes available, that's fine, but there are some do's and don'ts.

Please, please, please DON'T use sheets of A4 paper with a full script.

That's because with A4, you'll look like you couldn't be bothered to prepare the speech and that you had someone else write it for you. The sheets will flap around and distract people. You also risk looking like you're giving a lecture.

Do, do, do use flashcards. They should be small and discreet, listing just the key words/phrases you need to refer to.

This is where use of personal stories really reaps dividends. Just like when you're in the pub having a chat with your friends, stories are much easier to recount. We simply 'talk about them' rather than learn and recite them line by line.

Put the flashcards on the table in front of you. This can work well, provided you've practiced the speech this way, so you know you will be glancing down at them from time to time, not staring down at them.

Your eye contact with the audience is really important.

If you think back to the structure we talked about earlier, I suggest you use no more than seven cards.

That's one for each section which, if you remember, runs as follows:

- Build Rapport

- Establish Direction

- Key Point 1

- Key Point 2

- Key Point 3

- Groom's Great Gift

- Toast!

In reality, you'll probably find you don't need a card for the very first and last sections. I'll leave that for you to decide.

How to Practice

Another common question I regularly get asked is:

"How can I possibly memorise an entire speech?"

Let's take the 'memorisation' bit first.

Don't do it.

What?

That's right. *Don't memorise.*

What you're looking to do is 'internalise' your speech. In other words, to become so familiar with the speech that you find yourself almost 'talking about it' rather than reciting it.

What's the difference?

Well 'learning' a speech involves committing each word of each line to memory.

By contrast, internalising means being absolutely clear on the overall flow, so that each section of the speech transitions smoothly into the next. This frees you to talk *about* your speech, just as you would when having a drink with friends. You'll be far more natural that way and it's more engaging for your audience too.

To internalise your speech, I suggest you 'stage' your run-throughs. My own experience is that the variety is helpful – by using a number of different techniques for internalising the speech (rather than just staring-at-the-page mode) you internalise better.

Each stage is quite distinct from the others.

Stage 1: Reading

Stand up with your full script and read it out loud. Get used to how the script sounds, familiarise yourself with the flow but don't worry about eye contact.

Once you've done this a few times, you may well identify a few sections which you can improve to sound more natural. Crucially, it needs to 'sound like you' rather than like a robot.

How would you say it in real life? That's your litmus test.

Stage 2: Glancing

As before, only this time take your eyes off the page from time to time. You should keep doing this until you can read the speech by glancing at the script, rather than staring at it!

You should find that you can now put the script on a table in front of you and speak with even less reference to the script. Do this enough times and parts of the speech will begin to STICK in your mind.

Stage 3: Carding

Transfer your A4 script onto cue cards. By this stage, you should not need the *entire* script on the cards, just the key points, sufficient to jog your mind.

In time, you'll find that parts of the speech just come to you.

Stage 4: Recording

Record your speech onto your phone or audio device. Once you've got a draft you're happy with, listen to it and speak alongside.

Just like the lyrics of a song, if you speak along with your recording, you'll find yourself further internalising the flow. Notice also that there's no rule book which states you have to be sitting at a desk to follow this process. If you're like me, you might even go out for a jog!

Staging and Mechanics

I always like to know the exact place from which I'll be speaking. It may be a conference stage, a lecture theatre podium, or the table at a dinner,

Where will *you* be speaking from?

Sounds an obvious question. But this is worth checking out in advance, even if it's only just before dinner starts. Find out where and then spend some time there.

You should, if possible, position yourself in the exact spot. That way, you can get a feel for what it's like to be in that space. Later, when it comes to giving your speech, you'll find it easier because you've been there before.

If you're using props or visual aids, you'll want to ensure those are all set up as early as possible. This will minimise the amount of last minute rushing around you need to do.

Remember to brief people in advance if you need their help with uncovering a prop or adding to your speech in some way.

Microphones

There are different types but the most common are the lapel mic (attached to your jacket) and the handheld, which speaks for itself.

At weddings, lapel mics are rare in my experience, but if you're using one, the sound technician will want to talk to you beforehand to fit it and hopefully to do a sound check too. So you'll need to allow time for that.

With the handheld, remember you'll need to hold the mic closer to your mouth than feels comfortable. Just watch singers and comedians for an example of this.

Also remember that you need to have the mic directly in front of your mouth when you're speaking.

If you turn your head to one side, then the sound is lost. So, make sure the mic follows your mouth.

A word of caution here. Expect the unexpected! In my speech, the handheld mic conked out halfway through. You can see this happen on YouTube! If something does go wrong during your speech (for example, your mic may fail, a chair collapse or a siren go off) you've got two, and only two, options.

Option 1: ignore it and carry on.

Option 2: acknowledge what's happened and, if appropriate, make a joke about it.

In my case, when the mic failed, I went for Option 1. I put the mic down and carried on. But the audience applauded. How cool is that!

Occasionally, a speaker can get caught like a rabbit in

headlights. They stop, look a bit panicked and then try to decide what to do. My advice is to commit one way or the other. Either ignore the incident or make a feature of it.

The same is true with any unplanned distractions which occur during your speech.

Some years ago, I was listening to a speech by W Mitchell, a very experienced and impressive speaker, when a mobile phone went off in the audience.

Everyone could hear it.

The speaker decided to acknowledge it:

"If that's for me, tell them I'm not available. Unless it's Judy, I'll talk to Judy."

Brilliant! Again, the audience applauded.

If things *do* go wrong, think of it as an opportunity to have a laugh with the audience, rather than as a problem.

Relax, go with the flow and your audience will too.

7th Key - Summary

Top tips for handling the practicalities of your speech:

- Speak without notes for a stronger audience connection

- If using notes, go with flashcards not sheets of A4

- One card per section of your speech

- Internalise, don't memorise

- Use the Stage system to build your familiarity with the speech

- Establish where you will speak from

- Spend time there before your speech

- Keep mic to mouth

- If hit by sound problems, ignore or acknowledge

Epilogue

So, that's it!

You've now got all the Keys you need to develop and deliver a cracking Best Man Speech. I congratulate you on taking the time and trouble to invest in this book.

If you read and apply even 10% of what's contained within, you'll make a big difference to your speech.

Remember, your success is defined not by how funny you are or by making The Groom look a prat. Success is defined by paying heartfelt tribute to a man who, when asked to nominate a true friend, chose YOU.

Make The Parents proud and guarantee yourself success on the big day. Whatever friends may tell you, weddings are celebrations, not humiliations!

Be clear on the Key Points you want to make about The Groom. Select the best stories you can that illustrate those Points. Say something glowing about The Groom and about the couple.

Most importantly, go out there and sock it to 'em!

GOOD LUCK.

Appendices

Top tips from this book

The author's best man speech - a transcript

The world of public speaking
- from amateur to professional

Recommended resources

Top Tips from this book

Here in one place is a distilled list of the key tips and techniques outlined in the book...

- Avoid internet gags

- Focus on delivering a speech to delight The Parents, not The Friends

- Identify The Groom's 'Great Gift'

- Identify additional raw qualities (good or bad) of The Groom

- Have a chat with The Groom, Bride, Family & Friends, as appropriate

- Dig for stories during these conversations

- Keep a note!

- Identify core Themes

- Identify an overarching 'Big Theme' for the speech if one emerges

- Draft the Toast, then The Groom's Great Gift

- Decide on your 3 Key Points and identify relevant stories to illustrate

For effective storytelling:

- Give a brief context

- Identify a Critical Moment in the story

- Use dialogue!

- When drafting, allow only one sentence per line!

For humour, use...

- Setup-Punch

- Toppers

- Callbacks

For nerves...

- Think adrenaline, not nervousness

- Remember the audience doesn't know how nervous you are!

- Tip chin to chest, breathe deeply

- Use your neutral stance

- Drink something sweet

- Practice *out loud* & turn up the volume!

- Deliver with cards, not A4 (without notes, ideally)

- Internalise, don't memorise!

- Identify where you'll be speaking from - *before* your speech.

The author's Best Man speech **A transcript**

Ladies and gentlemen…

Sometimes you just get that feeling…

That you've got two people destined to get along with one another.

And I can still remember the night when Will first told me about Hannah.

He said: "Guess what, I've met someone!"

Well, that's a good start.

"Her name's Hannah… and I'm very excited about her."

Naturally, as a friend of his, I was intrigued.

Wouldn't you be?

What's she like?

How will she cope… with this man?

And are they well suited?

Imagine my relief when I learnt that Hannah is a specialist in working...

With difficult children.

That's right, right from the start I knew they were destined to get along just fine!

I should say that Rich and I have both been presented with a challenge in these two speeches.

At the start of the meal today, we were presented with five random words, selected by the ushers, which we're required to insert into our speeches without the audience noticing.

So I would invite you to look out during the course of what follows for those five words.

I obviously shan't tell you when they come.

It'll be up to you to spot them.

But just to give you a hint in the right direction, the words are: 'crocodile', 'semi-naked', 'moist', 'beaver' and 'anti-disestablishmentarianism'.

Now Will, as many of you will know, works in recruitment.

And very successful he is too.

And having worked in the industry myself, what I'm always struck by, when it comes to the world of recruitment, is the similarity between the recruitment game and the courtship game.

Many may enter the race, but there's only one job in the end.

So first, bearing in mind the extensive, rigorous application process – selection process I should say – that William had to progress through in order to win Hannah's hand in marriage...

First consider the application form.

Now on paper, Wim's credentials are impeccable.

A Forces background, with relatives involved in the army and the RAF.

Public school educated, a bastion of the establishment, a degree in Classics & Drama, a talent for acting.

With those credentials, with this pedigree, consider could this man... be a spy?

I invite you to consider the possibility that the man you thought you knew is but a myth.

An illusion.

A conjuror.

A master in the art of concealment.

Qualities of good taste, discretion, and irreproachable manners...

Concealed by this man for years.

But Hannah was not to be deceived.

Shrewd Hannah took a reference.

And I have in fact dug up just recently and have with me here today none other than a reference taken from William's former housemaster Mr Duncan Langlands.

Edited excerpts obviously but something broadly along the lines as follows...

"Just tell me where that boy is!"

It being a family wedding, I'll leave out some of the words that follow.

"Just because he's left school doesn't mean I've forgiven him for what he did to Mrs Langlands' rhododendron bush."

Hannah was impressed by this gardening prowess and so progressed Wim to the next stage of the process.

The oral interview.

You'll be pleased to hear that he skipped the 'group stage' of the courtship process.

Keen as ever to make a good first impression, Wim opted for the suave, sophisticated approach.

"Hey babe, take a look at my big ones!"

Referring of course to the two 850 page hardback fantasy novels tucked into his trousers.

Impressed by his passion for reading, Hannah enquired about Wim's skills as a communicator.

Thereby hitting on arguably the Groom's greatest strength.

His ability to speak!

Without doubt this man's greatest strength.

He gave some examples, a wealth of relevant experience.

Take for example the time when he was temping for a telesales agency.

Flogging photocopiers to small businesses.

In Dusseldorf.

Again, Hannah was impressed.

"I didn't know you spoke German!"

"I don't."

"So how did you communicate?"

"I asked them if they spoke English."

"And if they didn't, you…"

"Put the phone down."

One of this nation's greatest linguists.

But you wouldn't know it.

You wouldn't know it.

And there's more because buried deep within this man is an unbridled passion, energy, drive and thirst, appetite for hard work.

Artfully concealed.

Take for example the time when William was home alone, considering what to prepare for dinner.

But couldn't face the prospect of that treacherous two minute walk to the local shops.

As luck would have it the doorbell rang.

And who do you think should be standing there on the doorstep.

A semi-naked, cross-breed crocodile-beaver.

Of antidisestablishment views.

Moist because it was raining.

His response: "I'll have no truck with your anti-disestablishmentarianist views! Be on your way!"

Five minutes later the doorbell rang again.

This time it was a frozen food salesman.

Very cold the man was.

Selling bulk products at a discount price.

Consider the dilemma, ladies and gentlemen.

On the one hand, a treacherous two minute walk to the local shops to buy food, fraught with danger.

And on the other hand, thirty-six chicken kievs at £50 a pop.

Ladies and gentlemen, when this man is in the kitchen, it's chicken tonight.

And tomorrow night.

And the night after that.

But for all these powers of concealment, there is one quality that I've yet to mention.

A quality which he has never hidden.

And one which Hannah spotted early in the process.

Loyalty.

Loyalty to his friends.

And loyalty to those he loves.

Truth is ladies and gentlemen, in fifteen years of knowing this man, I've never known any man more loyal and more true than this man.

In fifteen years, I've seen it with other people and I've also been the beneficiary and I've experienced it myself in the times when he has been there for me.

William Rowe, a true friend.

[END OF VIDEO RECORDING]

Note: this transcript denotes the speech as viewable on youtube – it does not include the closing moments of the speech which contain The Toast. This was delivered in standard fashion by inviting the audience to be upstanding and raise their glasses to the Bride & Groom...

The world of public speaking

– from amateur to professional

People often ask me how I 'got into' public speaking as a career. The answer is: part design, part accident.

Back in May 2001, I had a nightmare speaking experience at my leaving drinks from my first job. At least, I thought it was a nightmare. Asked to give a speech without preparation, I froze up and felt terrible.

I managed to blurt out a few words – and talking to the audience members afterwards, they seemed very relaxed. But I wasn't. Far from it. I found the experience truly awful. This was not because I 'hated' speaking in front of audiences. In fact, from drama at school I knew that being in front of an audience was something I could quite enjoy.

What I found difficult was handling the adrenaline.

Anyway, to cut a long story short, I made a decision:

"Simon, sunshine, you've GOT to get better at this."

So, I went in search of safe environments in which I could practice. Think of it as a bit like being on a quest for a decent gym membership – only for communication skills, not physical fitness.

Eventually, in early 2004, I was introduced to Toastmasters International – a global network of not-for-profit public speaking clubs. Having checked out a few different clubs around London, I found one which I liked and, importantly, was conveniently located near Victoria Station, close to my place of work at the time.

The great strength of a Toastmasters speaking club is that not only does it provide an environment in which to practice, but also you receive constructive feedback from a fellow club member.

By this I mean *properly* constructive, quite unlike the harsh, negative and fundamentally unhelpful feedback so often provided in the workplace.

For the first two years of my membership, I was a member just like everyone else. Meetings were held twice a month on the first and third Monday. I'd pitch up and do a topic (Toastmasters jargon for 'impromptu speech'), fulfill a role or deliver a short prepared speech from my speaker's manual.

I must emphasise that I joined the club purely for my own personal development. The prospect of 'going professional' hadn't even entered my mind. Indeed, like most people, I assumed that 'professional speaking' was only really open to former Presidents, Prime Ministers, celebrities and Olympic gold medalists.

But as a result of a supportive speaking environment, surprise surprise, I improved rapidly, in confidence if nothing else. When I started out in January 2004, I was absolutely convinced I would never be able to speak without notes, yet within six months, that's precisely what I did. Delivering a 7 minute speech without recourse to a single scrap of paper was one of the proudest moments of my amateur speaking career.

Each year, 26,000 speakers around the world enter the Toastmasters International Speech Contest – a.k.a the 'World Championship of Public Speaking'.

Each contestant has 7 minutes to deliver a speech on any topic. A panel of judges decide on the winner who progresses to the next round in the competition. In my case, the trajectory was as follows:

Round 1 - London Cardinals Club Contest

Round 2 - Area 6 Contest (central London)

Round 3 - Division B Contest (London Final)

Round 4 - District 71 Contest (UK & Ireland Final)

Round 5 – Inter-District Contest (best of 7 Districts)

Round 6 – World Final

The Inter-District 'Semi-Final' and World Final itself are held each year at the International Convention, usually held in North America.

By spring 2006, I felt ready to enter the contest, not with any intention of winning of course, but simply to learn from the experience. And who knows? Perhaps I might scrape a win in my club contest?

Tentatively, in March 2006, I entered the London Cardinals Club contest with a speech about a bully from my school days – a bully who became a friend.

Put simply, the speech just kept winning!

By May, I was representing London in the UK & Ireland District Final in Mullingar, Ireland. By this stage, you're talking about audiences in the realm of 300-500 strong. The prize? A place in the Inter-District Semi-Finals to be held that year in Washington DC.

Sharing an emotive story with an audience is always a challenge. In my case, it was a story which blended childhood hatred, an ogre of a Headmaster, fights in the backyard, a poison pen letter informing an 8 year old boy that his parents were separating and a hand of friendship and support offered by the last person on earth I could ever have expected.

To tell that tale in the UK & Ireland Final, with my parents in the audience, was an experience I shall always remember. It was also a significant stepping stone towards the world of professional speaking.

Partly, that's because it gave me confidence in what I was capable of achieving with an audience. Perhaps more importantly, it gave me a profile within the amateur speaking community, which was to prove vital in the months ahead.

While I just missed out on the World Final, my experience was enough to attract the interest of Club Presidents across southern England. So, on my return from the USA, I had plenty of opportunities to visit clubs as a guest speaker... for free!

Then one day, the phone rang:

"Simon, I know you through Toastmasters – and I loved your contest speech. Look, we're seeking an MC for our business convention in June. I was wondering whether you'd like to do the role? I think you'll be great, but to be frank with you, we're also hoping you'll be cheap..."

Well, at least he was honest!

But I've never looked back.

While some people may have you believe otherwise, earning decent income through professional speaking is not an overnight phenomenon. It takes time.

Simply having great content or a terrific story to tell is not enough, I believe, to guarantee success with audiences. It's vital to have had enough experience (or 'stage time' as 2001 World Champion of Public Speaking, Darren LaCroix puts it) in front of audiences to know how to put your material across in a compelling way and to build a reputation as someone worth booking.

The fact that Best Men often struggle with speeches is not surprising given that, for many, it's the first time they'll have given a speech to an audience of that size.

What continues to shock me is the number of either very senior – or very visible – individuals, across all walks of life, who fail to engage an audience... when they should know better.

Malcolm Gladwell speaks of 10,000 hours – an investment of time which I completed quite a while ago in this field. If you're a Best Man reading this, rest assured, you won't need that in order to deliver a cracking 10 minute speech!

But for anyone seeking to pursue public speaking more seriously – either as a component of their work or as a full-time professional – I cannot overemphasise the value and importance of finding an environment in which you can hone your material, gain feedback and progress.

That needn't necessarily be a public speaking club, though that's what worked for me. There are countless associations, clubs and organisations in need of speakers. They may not pay a fee, but they offer something equally if not more valuable: first-hand experience and a pathway to improvement.

So, whether you're seeking a career in professional speaking, or you're interested in public speaking purely as a hobby, seek out opportunities to speak.

Hone your material, take a deep breath and go get 'em!

Recommended resources

The Six Minutes Blog

Probably the best - and certainly most comprehensive - public speaking blog that's out there. Search on the website under 'Best Man speech' and you'll find a short supplementary article written by the author on the topic.

www.sixminutes.dlugan.com

'How To Develop Self-Confidence And Influence People By Public Speaking' – Dale Carnegie

Not his most famous work but when it comes to public speaking, it's certainly one of the most humane and insightful. A timeless classic.

'Lend Me Your Ears' – Professor Max Atkinson

Again, while not specific to wedding speeches, contains a wealth of insight into the art of crafting a more compelling and effective speech or presentation.

2001 World Champion of Public Speaking – Darren LaCroix

Started public speaking as a way to improve his stand-up comedy. Now an expert on how to introduce humour more effectively into presentations. A very significant personal influence on the author. Highly recommend any resources by Darren.

Toastmasters International

If you're willing to invest some time, there's no better form of 'gym membership' for improving your public speaking. More than 10,000 clubs worldwide, most of which are open to all. You can attend as a guest free of charge. You won't be the first Best Man to join a club because you have a wedding speech to prepare!

www.toastmasters.org

Acknowledgements

A huge thank you to all those who have shaped my development as a speaker over the years. Many may recognize their influences in sections of this book. I am especially grateful to Toastmasters International, which first opened up the opportunity to develop my public speaking skills in a safe environment.

Members of my 'home public speaking club', London Cardinals Toastmasters, and in particular Nigel and Gilly Cutts, remain tremendous supporters and friends. I feel very grateful. Thank you for your mentoring, generosity of spirit and advice. Meanwhile, the club continues to offer an extraordinarily positive environment in which to develop as a speaker.

Others to whom I owe a debt of gratitude include: Darren LaCroix, Craig Valentine, Freddie Daniells, Dalice Trost, Richard Mullender, Lynne Cantor, Alex Ashworth, Maryam Pasha, Sue Cliff, Graham Jones, Dallas Leigh-Hill, Charlotte Hindle, James Marshall, Lee Warren, Sofie Sandell, Martina Strack, Ed Tate, Tom Salmon, David Issott, Ian Sheldon, Calum Miller, Will Butler, Debbie Salmon, James Micklethwait, Agnes Costa-Correa, James Kitto, Philip Bowen, Julian Foord and Ed Horner.

Thank you also to the many clients over the years, including the countless Best Men. It has been, and remains, a privilege to work with you.

A special thanks to my parents, James and Eileen – their combined support over the years has gone well beyond the call of parental duty. Quite simply (and literally) without them, none of this would have been possible. I am more grateful than I shall ever be able to put into words. What's more, in my mother, I am fortunate to have perhaps the most assiduous proof-reader on the planet.

Needless to say, any errors, omissions or grounds for offence that lie within this book are mine – and mine alone... and more than likely down to my impatience.

Finally, to Jenny, Freya and Isaac - you're tremendous.

About the Author

In 2005, Simon Bucknall told an emotional tale from his school days to an audience in a small London pub. Six months later, with that same speech he won the UK & Ireland Championship of Public Speaking. He went on to place in the top 20 out of 26,000 speakers worldwide.

A full-time professional keynote speaker, masterclass facilitator and coach since 2008, Simon helps high-achieving professionals, leaders and opinion formers to connect, influence and inspire through the spoken word. In addition to numerous Best Men and wedding speakers, Simon's clients include corporate executives, MBAs, PhDs, politicians, charity workers, entrepreneurs and young people in schools.

Simon was invited to be Best Man for a close friend from school a matter of weeks before flying to the USA to represent the UK & Ireland in the finals of the World Championships of Public Speaking. He has been coaching Best Men and wedding speakers ever since. On youtube, video footage of Simon's Best Man Speech has exceeded 118,000+ hits and is still rising. It remains one of the most popular wedding speeches on the web.

Simon is a Fellow of the UK Professional Speaking Association and the Royal Society for the Arts. He is also a Visiting Fellow of London's New College of the Humanities. He holds degrees from Oxford University and the London School of Oriental & African Studies and is a Freeman of the City of London.

Simon lives in London with his wife and family.

the art of connect
ion

Communication skills expertise for high-achieving professionals, leaders and opinion formers.

Whether you're presenting at a conference, pitching for new business or seeking to impress senior colleagues, when you speak, your credibility is at stake.

The Art Of Connection offers masterclasses, coaching and keynote talks to help YOU achieve the impact you need.

Formats include:

- Half-day, 1-Day & 2-Day Masterclasses
- One-to-One Coaching
- Keynote Talks
- Public Events
- Away Days & Residential Events

Expertise covers public speaking & presentation skills, listening skills, assertiveness, influence & persuasiveness skills, interview skills & voice coaching.

If you would like to find out more, please contact us at:

info@theartofconnection.co.uk

www.theartofconnection.co.uk

Printed in Great Britain
by Amazon